For the new 9-1 GCSEs

UPGRADE YOUR GRADES

ROHAN GUPTA

Notion Press

Old No. 38, New No. 6
McNichols Road, Chetpet
Chennai - 600 031

First Published by Notion Press 2019
Copyright © Rohan Gupta 2019
All Rights Reserved.

ISBN 978-1-68466-9-264

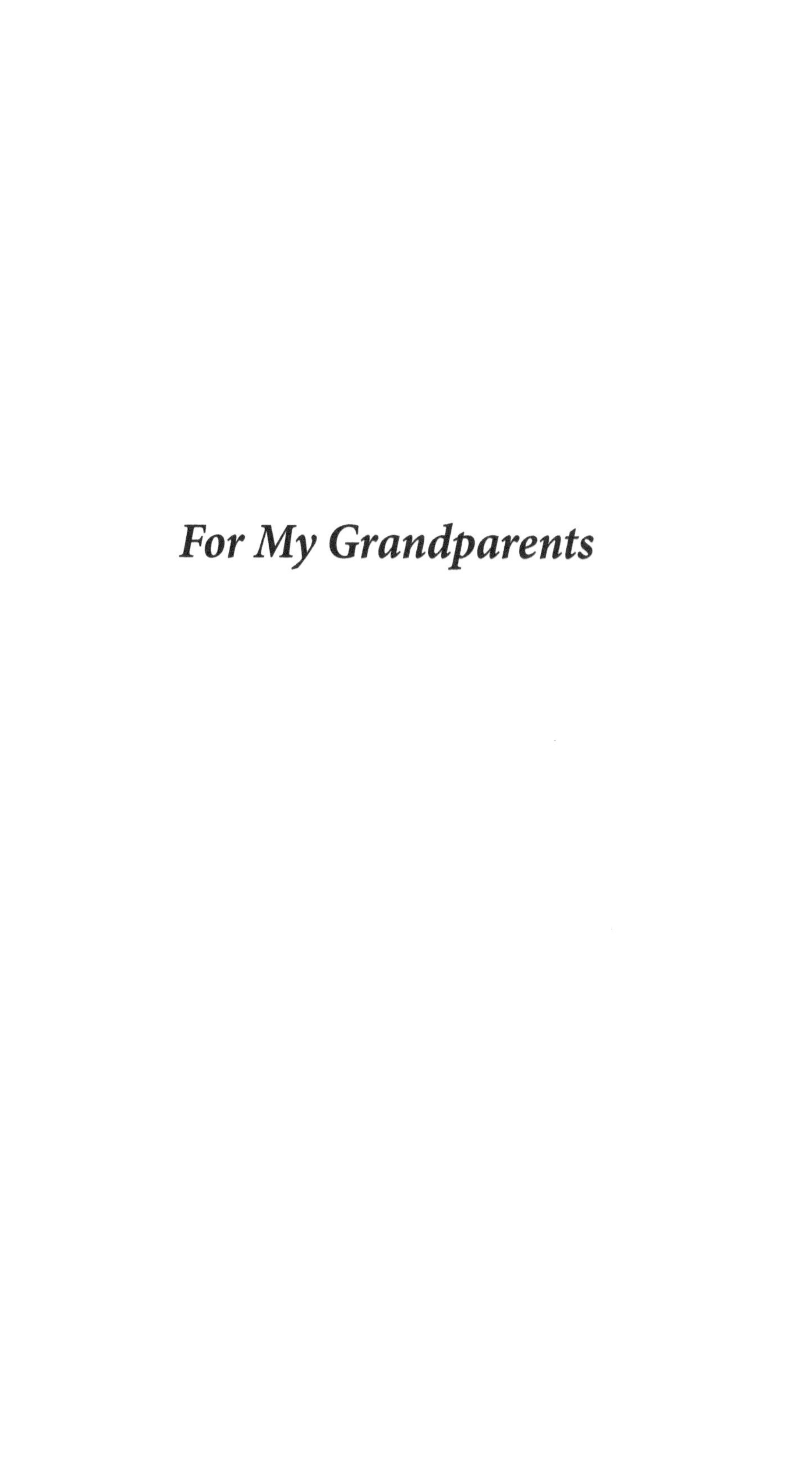

For My Grandparents

Contents

Preface

I completed my GCSEs last year. Currently I am studying Maths, Further Maths, Physics and Economics at A level. Straight after my GCSEs, in the summer holidays I decided to pen down my revision techniques and planning methods which helped me achieve my goals. Hopefully my younger sister, Riya, and numerous other students will benefit from this and achieve their potential.

I would like to thank my aunt, Neena Chandra, for editing this book. She has made valuable suggestions and improvements thus making the book ready for publication.

I would like to thank my parents for inspiring me to write.

Introduction

My name is Rohan. At the time of writing, I am 16 years old and have just finished my GCSEs and I achieved seven 9s, three A*s and an A.

I have been an average student in a school in Hull, in the North of England. I would prefer to play sports such as badminton and cricket to studying. But I did want to go to a good university so I could get a good job. So for my GCSEs, I started working really hard. One big problem is that there's very little information available on exam preparation. Every website you look at will give you some ideas, such as making a revision plan, but won't explain how to do them effectively.

After I got my results, I started writing my approach to GCSE exams to help future students to attain their best through my techniques. Therefore, I decided to produce a clear guide on how to get through your GCSEs, and attain your full potential.

In this book, I have written all the useful tips I collected, which helped me to get top grades. It is designed exclusively for GCSE students taking the new 9–1 syllabus as I was amongst the first students to take them.

When I learnt about the GCSE reforms, I immediately felt anxious. When we asked what the reason for the change was, we were told that *too many students are getting good grades and passing with flying colours.* What a ridiculous reason to change the curriculum!

The changes were a shock and there was so much uncertainty – the sheer workload itself had become so vast that tackling it was a challenge in itself. I couldn't believe how much we had to do.

We had new textbooks, we followed new syllabi and had no past papers to solve. This made life much harder for all of us.

THE NEW 9–1 GCSES

Some GCSE subjects changed from A*-G in 2017, and the rest in 2018.

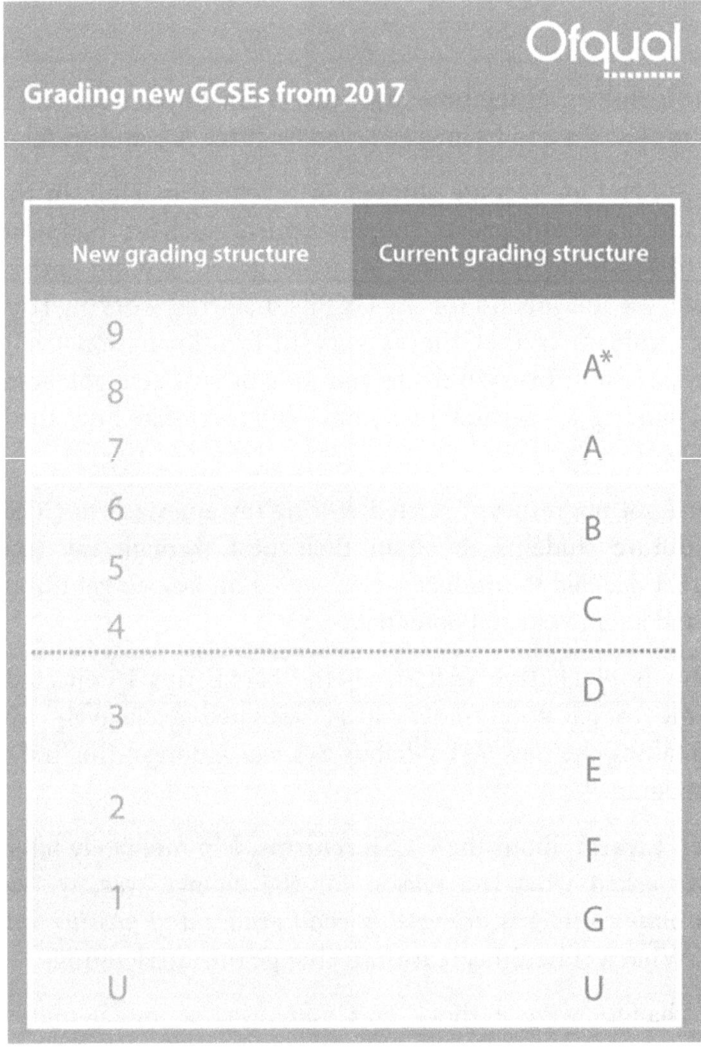

The new courses are more challenging than ever, with all the exams set at the end of Year 11.

Grade 4 is now considered a 'Standard Pass.'

Grade 5 is a 'Good Pass.'

A* is now split into 8 and 9, so achieving the highest grade has become much harder. Only the top 20% of students with Grades 7, 8 or 9 will get 9.

Only 732 students in the whole country got a clean sweep of all 9s this year.

Finally, coursework and practical assessments play a much smaller part in the new GCSE courses—which means most of the marks are won or lost in the exams at the end of Year 11, making the final exams much more important than ever before.

WHY ARE GCSES IMPORTANT?

The transition from Year 9 to Year 10 may be the biggest transition you've experienced so far. One year life is relaxed with no academic pressure, and the next year everybody's telling you how hard you have to work. This *is* an intimidating experience, for anybody.

This is the time when you need to start thinking about the future. At the moment you may just want to play video games with your friends, but in the future, you're going to want to go to one of the top universities and get a well-paid, and respected, job. Don't let the GCSEs become your biggest regret in future life.

There are 4 main ways in which your GCSE results are going to affect you:

1. Entry requirements for sixth forms vary – ranging from grade 5's, through to grade 7's for the most selective colleges. Being accepted into a good 6th form improves your chances of getting into the top universities.

2. Universities look at your GCSE grades to decide whether or not to give you an offer, for example:

    a. To study Management at the University of Leeds, you need at least grade 6's in English Language and Maths.

    b. To study Psychology at the University of Bath, you need at least grade 7's in the majority of your subjects.

    c. To study Law at Manchester Metropolitan University, you need a grade 4 in English Language.

    d. To study Medicine, Dentistry or Veterinary Medicine anywhere, you'll need at least 7's in most of your subjects.

3. GCSEs have become more important than ever before due to the reduction in schools doing AS levels at the end of Year 12. This means the only external exam results universities will be able to look at before making an offer, are your GCSEs. Also, you shouldn't just aim for the minimum possible grade requirements given as it makes it unlikely that you'll get the place. For example, if you require grade 7's to get into a course, but the university has

15 applicants for every seat, they will tend to choose the students with grade 8s or 9s.

4. Many high paying jobs ask for minimum GCSE grades in English and Maths.

Take a look at the figures below, published by the Office of National Statistics, showing how earnings vary with the qualifications you attain.

Data summary

Average hourly pay - 2010
Click heading to sort - Download this data

Qualification	Median hourly pay (£)	Pay gap to GCSE, %
Degree	16.10	85
Higher education	12.60	45
A Levels	10.00	15
GCSE grades A*-C	8.68	0
Other qualifications	8.07	-7
No qualification	6.93	-20

SOURCE: ONS

This clearly shows that those with GCSE passes earn 20% more than those without them.

COMMON EXCUSES TO OVERCOME

The two most common excuses which lead people to failure are:

1. My school isn't good enough

2. I'm not good enough

If any of these are things you've thought to yourself before, read this chapter carefully. If not, you can skip to the next one.

There are 2 types of people. There are those who believe what happens in their life is caused by external factors which they can't control, and there are those who believe they can control their lives.

You Need to Believe You Can Control Your Life.

If you believe you can't control what happens, you have no incentive to work hard for your GCSEs, and you fail before even starting.

My School Is Not Good Enough

The problem with the school environment is that the clever people are often at the bottom of the social ladder, while the ones who don't care about studying are the 'cool' ones. This creates an incentive for you to stop showing interest in class and to stop revising. This can be detrimental to your final result.

Instead, you need to remember that the ones who do well in GCSEs do better in life. Those who refuse to even try to learn anything will fail their GCSEs and end up at the bottom of the social ladder for the rest of their lives. This should become your incentive to work hard. Also, you don't need to tell anybody about your revision. Keep it to yourself and it doesn't have to affect your life at school.

As Bill Gates said: "Be nice to nerds. Chances are you'll end up working for one."

Another problem can be poor teaching. Some teachers are passionate about their subject but go off topic too much, some teachers are too slow and won't finish the entire syllabus in time, and some teachers just don't care. Some teachers give so much information and notes that you do not know where to start or finish.

You need to spend extra time doing work on those subjects. You need to realise that teachers are just a tool for you to reach your goals and you have plenty of other tools you can use if they're not good enough.

I'm Not Good Enough

The most common reason that people don't do enough revision is because of a lack of energy. You come home after a long Friday at school and decide that you're too tired to do anything and you'll just postpone any work you have to do till tomorrow. And then you sleep in on the weekend and don't have enough time to do it. That probably sounds familiar to you because I'm sure everyone has gone through that before.

My solution to this is to plan exactly how much revision you'll do beforehand and ensure you stick to your plan. Your plan can't be vague, it must be exact. If you plan to "do algebra for the whole evening" you'll probably do 3 questions before deciding that's enough. If you plan to "do 25 questions of algebra" then you can't persuade yourself to do any less.

Another common reason is believing you're not smart enough. My intelligence is just average. I don't grasp new concepts or memorise information very quickly or easily. It did annoy me when the 'naturally clever' people just read a chapter and seemed to understand it better.

Then I did my research. I discovered that there are three things which are important when it comes to learning, understanding and memorising information.

The most important aspect is your discipline. This is your ability to sit down at a table, start working and maintain your concentration, as well as your ability to avoid procrastinating. This is not something one can be born with, it's something that has to be acquired and strengthened – like a muscle.

Second most important is your revision technique. This is also something which you are fully in control of. If you don't already have a revision technique that works for you, I'll teach you some which you can test out and find out which is best for you.

Finally, your intelligence does play a role in how fast you can learn and assimilate information, but it has by far the smallest effect on your GCSE grades of the three.

Revision Technique

REVISION PLAN

The first thing you need to do, before even touching a textbook, is to make a **revision plan.** This keeps you going in the right direction, gives you confidence and stops you worrying while revising. Many people say "You could be spending that time revising instead of making a plan" but spending 1 or 2 evenings to make the plan has much greater overall benefits than spending that evening revising.

The real question is always "When should I start revising?." I would always recommend starting around 5 months before your first exam. Many students will only start revising in April but these students are going to be very stressed for two months and will almost certainly end up with worse grades than someone who started before. Also, the earlier you begin, the less work you have to do each day.

It's important that you revise each subject at least three times so that it sticks in your long-term memory. Each revision will be around twice as fast as the previous revision of that subject.

First Revision

Your first 'layer' of revision should be around three months. You should give 10–11 days for each subject. You can revise 1 subject at a time which is what I did, but if you know that you'll get bored doing that, you should revise a different subject every day so that you don't get bored, but only revise 1 subject per day.

This is an example timetable for your first 'layer' of revision if you decided to do your subjects one at a time.

Subject	Start Date	End Date	No. of Days
Geography	11-Dec	21-Dec	11
Chemistry	22-Dec	1-Jan	11
Physics	2-Jan	12-Jan	11
Biology	13-Jan	23-Jan	11
Maths	24-Jan	3-Feb	11
Computer Science	4-Feb	14-Feb	11
Business Studies	15-Feb	21-Feb	7
English Literature	22-Feb	4-Mar	11
English Language	5-Mar	15-Mar	11

One of your subjects might coincide with your half term holidays at school so you can do that for less time (like business studies which I gave 7 instead of 10 days). However, I gave chemistry the full 11 days despite being in the Christmas holidays because you'll end up using a few days playing with your new video games.

Layer one is the most important layer, and you can't rush it. At this stage, it's more important that you completely understand everything rather than learning it. If there's any topic you struggle with, you can't just skip past it. You need to reread it and if you still don't understand it, use some online resources like BBC Bitesize to understand it. If you still can't understand it, make a note of which topic it is and go see your teacher outside of lesson time.

Second Revision

Your second 'layer' of revision should be around one and a half months long. You should give 3–5 days to each subject. Here you must cover one subject at a time as it helps your brain to group subject information together and pick it up quickly in the exam.

This is an example timetable for your second 'layer' of revision.

Subject	Start Date	End Date	No. of Days
Geography	17-Mar	21-Mar	5
Chemistry	22-Mar	26-Mar	5
Biology	27-Mar	31-Mar	5
English Literature	1-Apr	5-Apr	5
Computer Science	6-Apr	10-Apr	5
Physics	11-Apr	15-Apr	5
Business Studies	16-Apr	20-Apr	5
English Language	21-Apr	25-Apr	5
Mathematics	26-Apr	30-Apr	5

At this stage, you should do a quick revision of the entire syllabus, and then start doing some past papers. **Don't do all the past papers as you'll need some for before the exam.**

Third Revision

Your third 'layer' of revision is your final revision just before exams, and in between exams. How much time you give to each subject varies depending on how your exam timetable is structured, but aim to give around 3 days to each subject. First, you should do a quick skim read of the textbook and then finish off as many past papers as you can.

WHAT TO REVISE?

There are many different sources of information that you can use such as your notes from your school exercise book, textbooks, revision guides and online resources. A major problem occurs when you try to use every resource at your disposal, as you'll go into 'information overload.' This is the biggest problem with teachers giving you loads of printed handouts. They expect you to 'soak it up like a sponge' when this isn't possible.

The source of information you should use depends completely on the subject. The main thing is that whatever you revise from, it should be specific to the exam board you're doing. Many textbooks are generic, meaning that you can use them for any exam board. You should never use these because a lot of the information in it will be irrelevant to you meaning that you have to do extra learning with no added benefit.

To get the grades you want, you need to ensure you learn as much relevant information as you can, in the least possible time. This means only using one, trustworthy, resource.

I'll go into more detail about what specifically to revise in the subject by subject advice.

HOW MUCH TO REVISE?

This is probably the hardest question to find an answer to. If you go online, all you'll find are "as much as you can." That's why, for my mocks, I did a maximum of 2 hours of revision every day. That wasn't enough for me to get the grades I wanted.

A good rule of thumb is that the number of hours per day you should revise in the Easter holidays is your target grade minus 2. For example, if you're aiming to get an 8, you should revise 6 hours a day in Easter. If you're aiming to get a 4, you'll be able to achieve that with 2 hours of revision per day.

By knowing beforehand how many hours of revision you'll do per day, it makes breaking down your revision much easier. For example, let's say you're in your third layer and need to finish the whole biology course in 3 days. First, check how many pages there are in the textbook (mine has 342). Then divide this by 3 so you know you're doing about 114 pages per day. Then divide this by the number of hours you're going to revise (e.g. 7, if you're aiming for a grade 9) so you'll do about 16 pages per hour.

You can then take a break for the rest of the hour after you've finished these 16 pages. The only problem with this is that you may rush yourself to finish them so you can have a break. Make sure you don't do that as it'll render your revision redundant.

Overall, this makes revision so much less stressful. Revising 16 pages per hour doesn't sound nearly as bad as revising the entire biology syllabus in just 3 days. However, you don't always have to revise exactly 16 pages per hour. Try to finish off a chapter if it's around 16 pages. For example, chapter 1b in my textbook is 19 pages, so instead of leaving 3 pages for the next hour, I would just finish chapter 1b in one sitting.

HOW TO REVISE?

Everyone has their own revision methods that they swear by. For a large number of people, it is making notes from the textbook. For others, it is reading a revision guide and for some, it can even be things like reading it out in funny accents.

All of these methods will work; however, some are more efficient than others, and I am going to go through advantages and disadvantage of each one before telling you which combination of methods I believe is the best.

Method 1 – Note Taking

Many people like to open their textbook from page one, keep some lined paper, colourful highlighters and gel pens handy, and then start rewriting the textbook onto their paper as neatly as they can.

One advantage of this is that people find it very easy to simply read and then write it, and the information simply gets stored in your head. Another advantage is that this method seems like fun because of all the colouring or highlighting you get to do.

However, both of these are also disadvantages. Research shows that you find it easy because after around 5 minutes of doing it, your cerebral cortex activity decreases and you stop thinking about doing it. Then it can become partly subconscious like breathing; you stop thinking about doing it and you just do it. This is a problem when revising because you can think you've revised a full chapter when in reality you've just mindlessly copied the information from one place to another.

It's also very time consuming, partly because writing everything out so neatly takes time, but also because people spend a lot of time highlighting and colouring when this doesn't actually help you remember it much at all.

Most people will then file these notes away in a folder and keep them organised for later revision, but given that you have a textbook with all the information you need, what's the point of making notes? What makes it worse is that you try to summarise all the information, you lose some information from the textbook, making this system very inefficient. Considering your exam could ask anything in the textbook, how do you choose what to write down and what to ignore? This means when you walk into the exam, you won't have learnt all the necessary information.

Method 2 – Reading from Revision Guides

A lot of people get intimidated by having to open a 400 page textbook and learn everything, so they turn to a 100 page revision guide. They're less intimidating, they're colourful and often filled with pictures and jokes, and best of all they claim that they teach you everything you need to know. In reality, they won't.

You shouldn't worry about the size of the textbook because if you divide it up into days, it becomes much easier for you to handle and you'll find yourself feeling much less stressed.

Guides try to filter a thick textbook into a thin little book, but in the process they miss out on important bits of information. These bits of information will add up and can mean the difference between getting the grade you want or a lower grade.

There is only one advantage to a revision guide, which is that it is very fast. This means it can be useful for your final revision when you need to finish an entire subject in a day.

The Ideal Mixture

In order to best memorise all the information, I would recommend using a mixture of 3 different revision methods, one for each layer. This method will work for most subjects, such as sciences and humanities, but won't for languages or maths. I'll tell you how to revise those in the subject by subject advice.

In your **first layer,** you have loads of time and you need to ensure that you understand everything in the book. That's why I recommend using note taking for this layer. However, don't do it the traditional way because of all the disadvantages I explained earlier. Instead, you should read a page of the textbook until you understand it, and then cover the page, wait 5–10 seconds and then write down as much of the information as you can. This forces your brain to learn, understand, hold and recall information very rapidly, a skill that will come in handy in the exam. Don't worry if you can't memorise all the information in one go. Just have another look at the page and do it again. If there's a piece of information that you struggle with both times or you don't understand, mark it with a star or underline it in the textbook so you are sure to pay extra attention to it next time.

Don't worry about writing it neatly and don't use colours. Your aim here is to use the note taking method, without it being so time-consuming. You're not going to be keeping these notes anyway, they're just a way for you to see what you've been able to memorise. You can throw them away after you've finished a subject.

In your **second layer,** I would suggest just reading your textbook. In this layer, you have less time so you may not be able to write everything down. I would still recommend using your textbook rather than a revision guide so that you're reminding yourself of all the information, rather than just bits of it. In this layer, you should answer questions from the textbook or a workbook, and also start doing past papers. Make sure you leave some past papers for layer 3.

Your **third layer** is your shortest and you need to be able to revise an entire subject in a day, with time to do past papers. In this, I'd recommend the "teaching" method. You need to find a family member willing to sit down and listen to you for a while and teach them the subject. This is the fastest way to do a comprehensive revision of the subject. If you don't have a family member free to do it, then you can just imagine there's a class in front of you and do it. In this layer, you need to have the specification in front of you while teaching so you don't miss any points. If there's something you're still stuck on, go back into the textbook and reread it two or three times to ensure you remember it. Finally, you need to finish off all the remaining past papers, preferably under timed conditions.

DAILY LIFE

When preparing for your GCSEs, you can't keep the same routine that you've probably had for the last few months or years. That means no watching Netflix until 2 a.m., and no sleeping in until lunchtime on weekends. You need to have a routine, and maintain discipline yourself. This is especially important on weekends, but first I'll run through weekdays with you.

Weekdays

On weekdays, I capped myself off at 40 minutes of TV a day, and an hour on my phone. You can set your own targets, but don't be too ambitious because you don't want to be suffering 'withdrawal symptoms' while revising. Also, set a specific time to go to sleep so that you are not sleep deprived as this makes revision much harder.

When you get back home after school, don't go straight to the TV. The first place you should go is your desk. Then, using the method I told you in "How to Revise" divide your day of work into a timetable for the day. Open up your textbooks to the correct page, get a snack and drink and start. I would often eat anchovies, sardines or mackerel because these oily fish contain OMEGA-3 which is good for your brain. While I can't be sure whether they actually helped me to revise, they definitely didn't have any negative effect. Also, avoid coke or any fizzy drinks at this time. Try to stick to water or fruit juice.

As I said before, make sure to divide your work up into hours, and if you finish the work before the hour ends, give yourself a well deserved break until the next revision hour starts.

Good things to do in your break are: exercise, eat a snack, browsing Instagram for a short time.

Bad things to do in your break are: Starting a movie, going on the Xbox or PS4, going out to do shopping or watching Youtube.

If you do decide to go on Instagram, Snapchat or Facebook in your break, set a timer for when you're going to finish as otherwise it's almost guaranteed that you're going to forget to start revising again.

Weekends

On weekends, try to ensure that you wake up when your alarm goes off and avoid sleeping in too late. I'm not suggesting you should wake up at 6 a.m., rather I'm trying to encourage you to wake up at 8.30 or 9 a.m. rather than 10 or 11 a.m. like you probably would want to.

The first thing you do in the morning (after eating breakfast) is to make a full plan of the day, dividing the amount of work that you need to do by the number of hours you can spend doing it. Then your day is set and you can just follow your plan. Ensure you eat every meal and have constant snacks and water as some people get so absorbed in their revision, they end up skipping meals.

KEEPING MOTIVATED

In this chapter, I will teach you effective motivation techniques and how to deal with de-motivating thoughts. This is designed to give you the ability to fight off procrastination and motivate yourself to study in evenings and weekends.

I believe motivation is simply the opposite of procrastination. In order to teach you how to keep motivated, I must also teach you how to fight procrastination. When you're highly motivated, you procrastinate less and when you're procrastinating a lot it means you're low on motivation.

Everyone has good days (where motivation is greater than procrastination) and bad days (where procrastination is greater than motivation).

On a good day, you will be well rested, cheerful and positive. You will probably be feeling confident and when you do start revising, your mind will be fully focused on what you're doing. You won't be worried about what's going to happen in the future and your desire to reach your targets will keep you working hard.

On a bad day, you might be tired due to lack of sleep the previous night. You may be complacent or overconfident, leading you to keep on pushing your revision start time a little later until, finally, you'll realise that you have to start working. By then, you'll have to do the entire workload in a short time, leaving you feeling overwhelmed. This can make you anxious that you won't finish, leading to negative thoughts about exam results. This can give you trouble concentrating, making your revision even worse. At this stage, if you get stuck on any questions or have trouble understanding a concept, you can lose confidence and get even more scared for your exam. Then the negative thoughts can start spiralling. Eventually, you'll realise that none of the revision you did that night actually went into your head. This can make you decide to stop working for the day and just try again tomorrow.

Everybody will have both good days and bad days just as I described above. The important thing is to have as many good days and as few bad days as possible. As you'll see, the triggers that start off a bad day are a bad night of sleep and overconfidence. To avoid these, sleep on time every night and always make sure you can feel the right amount of exam pressure. Not enough to make you overly anxious but just enough so that you feel like revising when you get the chance.

The first 10 minutes of revision are always the hardest to maintain concentration. Once you finish this, you should easily be able to have another 35 minutes of good study time without trying too hard. After this time, you may start to lose concentration. At this point, you may need to employ some extension strategies. These are some of my ideas to try to gain 5–10 more minutes of revision time before losing concentration.

Once you've done this, hopefully you'll have finished your hourly target and will be able to take a break. Even a short 5 minute break will allow you to do another 45 minutes of revision much more easily.

One 'extension strategy' is to keep handy a print of some motivational quotes by people you know, whether they're fictional, famous or just something a relative said to you, that you found inspiring. Whatever it is, look at it when you get close to the end of your concentration and use it as a springboard to get a little more motivation.

Another 'extension strategy' is to read in a different way. This could be reading it aloud instead of in your head, or it could be reading it in your head, with someone else's accent. This could be anyone too, a friend, a movie character, or a celebrity. I often used to use the subject teacher's voice, Batman's voice and even Arnold Schwarzenegger's voice occasionally.

Subject by Subject Advice

MATHS

A lot of people get extremely stressed about maths. I understand that if you don't understand it, it can be a daunting task, but you can and will make progress if you just keep at it. Don't try and avoid it, but also don't let it consume your life and affect the rest of your revision.

Before beginning any maths revision, ensure you have a good revision guide for your exam board and specification. CGP offer some great ones. These aren't going to be your main revision but whenever you get stuck or forget how to do something, this is what you'll turn to in order to revise by the correct method.

It's very important to carefully read through some worked examples which are in every maths revision guide to ensure that you fully understand every step of the process.

It's also very important to do lots of practice questions for maths. Practising what you've learnt is just as important as learning it because, in maths, it's the only way to consolidate the method firmly in your head. Test yourself by doing past papers and any questions in your textbook and revision guide. In maths, the person who completes the highest number of practice questions before the exam will almost always get the highest mark.

If there is any subject, any subject ever that you need to use past papers for, it's maths. Use old past papers, use specimen papers. Find any maths papers you can and just do them. This way, odds are that you'll recognise almost half the questions in your exam but they'll just be slightly changed. For example, I did Edexcel Maths and did the last 10 years of papers from the old specification, and found lots of similarities in the exam paper. Highlight any questions that you get wrong for future reference.

The main thing for maths is: practice, practice, practice. You just need to practice. You know the theory but you need to be able to apply it. Lots of people know all the methods but don't know what the questions are asking, especially with higher maths where they try to confuse you with weird questions.

Another great resource is MathsWatch. Most schools give students a MathsWatch account. The best advantage of this is that it's topic by topic, with worked examples fully explained and you can rewind it, pause it and play it again. I know the woman's voice is annoying but you just have to deal with it. If you haven't got a Mathswatch, ask your maths teacher to get you one, or ask a friend from another school for their login details.

There are also a few formulae, such as the quadratic formula, that you might have to learn. This varies with exam boards but over time, you will automatically learn it if you do it often enough. If you haven't been able to learn it or are really stressed about it, try writing it out on post it notes and sticking them around the house or your room. If you are doing this, be careful that you don't start ignoring the notes after a day or so. Make sure to read them carefully every time you pass one just to be sure.

With the above techniques and practice I was able to achieve 97% in the Maths GCSE.

The Maths Exam

One of the biggest problems with maths exams is the sheer number of silly mistakes that everybody makes. This is why it's very important to read every word of the question carefully and not make any assumptions. I know you're thinking "of course I wouldn't be dumb enough to skim read a GCSE Maths question" but in reality, our brains try to take shortcuts everywhere so if you've seen a similar question before, you may automatically assume it's basically the same thing. It might not be. Reread the question to be sure.

The good thing about maths exams is that they give you loads of time so that you can check through your paper at the end; take advantage of this and do it. Many people get bored after quickly checking their paper once and then they spend the rest of their time just rereading their exam paper. I'll admit that I did this too, but I shouldn't have. Imagine how disappointed you'd be if you didn't get the grade you wanted because you lost out by just a few marks because of a silly mistake that could have been spotted if you checked thoroughly.

In your second check, use your calculator for every possible sum just to be absolutely sure you haven't made any arithmetic errors. Even if the sum is 11+7, just do it in a calculator to be sure because the pressure of the exam can make your mental maths go off.

Always make sure your answer is in the format they're looking for. They will deduct a mark if you haven't converted cm to m, for example, or if you gave an answer to 4 significant figures when they asked for 3.

I'm sure your maths teacher has already parroted this to you hundreds of times, but always show your workings. Most questions only have 1 or 2 marks for the answer and all the other marks for the working out, so you could still get 4 marks on a 6 mark question with an incorrect answer, simply by showing how you got to it.

$$2 > -3 \qquad \infty \qquad \begin{matrix} + & - \\ \times & \div \end{matrix}$$

$$0.999\ldots = 1$$

$$\pi \approx 3.14 \qquad 5^2$$

$$\sqrt{2} \qquad 1 + 2 \cdot 3$$

$$(1 - 2) + 3$$

$$5(2 + 2) \qquad 101_2 = 5_{10}$$

ENGLISH

The most common excuse for English is that "You can't revise English." I used this excuse right up until my real GCSE exams, which is why I was so worried about how to revise English for the real thing. But it is very important that you revise English. In Year 10 and my mocks, I got a 7 in English Literature because I did absolutely no revision but after doing proper revision for my GCSEs, I managed to get a 9.

In English, memorising information before your exam won't get you all the marks like a science. You need to be able to write essays using correct spelling, punctuation, grammar and high level vocabulary.

You've probably learnt about PEE paragraphs from your teachers. This stands for Point, Evidence, Explanation. The point should be what you're trying to say; a concise answer to the question. Evidence should be a quote from the play or novel you're studying and the Explanation should tell the examiner exactly what the quote means and how it proves your point.

Most people take both English Literature and English Language. English Literature is much easier to revise. You have to make sure you have the right quotes for every character or theme they could throw at you, and have some analysis for it. Most text guides will give you just enough information to get a 4 or 5 in the exam, but if you want to get an 8 or 9, you'll need to listen in class all year round for Years 10 and 11 and make a note of everything the teacher says. Then your first job when revising is to arrange these notes into notes which you can revise from. You have to memorise the key quotes.

Some people can read a passage of a poem and easily understand all the hidden meanings the poet is trying to convey. I couldn't. The only thing I could do is try to impress the examiner with as many relevant quotes as I could write down, and then write how it answers the question.

For English Literature, reread your book again in April or May, but it's more important to revise quotes and their analysis than it is to just memorise the plot of the book.

English Language is much more difficult to revise for because they could ask you to answer virtually any question. For this, just practice doing transactional writings a few times and give them in to your teacher for marking. Ask them what advice they can give you to help you get the highest marks.

For the extracts, just revise what you've gone over in class again and check Amazon to see if there are any relevant guides. They must be board specific otherwise there's no point getting them.

English is unique in that it is entirely subjective and based on what the examiner thinks of your essay. However, your teachers will know what the examiner is looking for. This means it's extremely important in English that you're a part of each and every lesson as revision resources like textbooks in English aren't good enough for the highest grades.

SCIENCES

Everyone who does GCSE does science in one form or another. With the new GCSE specification, it's become a lot harder than it used to be, especially as you have to memorise a lot of formulae.

CGP revision guides are indispensable for science. I never actually touched my class notes while revising; all of my revision was done through CGP. CGP was my lifeline, but what's better than the Revision Guides are the Student Books. Firstly, they have a lot more detail than the revision guide which you'll need for a lot of the 4 or 6 mark questions. Secondly, each topic has the specification printed out on the side so you can have a mental checklist of each topic.

The Student Book was at least 85% of my revision for each science, with the other 15% being past papers.

There are past papers online going back to 2001. I know that the format is completely different to the current format, but a majority of the content is the same. If you come to a question you don't think is on your specification, just put a dot next to it and go into the index of your textbook to try and find it. If it's in there it means you need to revise that bit much more thoroughly.

If you're aiming to get an 8 or 9 in a science, then knowing exam technique is as important as learning the content. You could have fully learned the content but still come out with a 7 if you haven't understood exam technique.

The only way to get the feel of an exam and understand exam techniques is to do past papers in exam conditions. That means closed book, time limits and sitting on a chair at a desk with no distractions. It's very hard to do this every time; I admit that I often got too tired and went on my phone in the middle of a past paper but that's a bad thing which you should avoid if possible. Make sure that you treat it like an exam, giving it your full focus and effort.

When you're marking, be harsh on yourself. Keep all your past papers in a folder for future reference.

Try and notice trends and patterns within past papers as it'll help you in the real exam. This is what differentiates an 8/9 student from a 6 or below student.

MODERN LANGUAGES

For my modern language, I chose Spanish because I found it to be far easier than French, but the way of revising any language is the same. Vocabulary. Every exam board's language specification has a list of words in the language and English that you need to know. The single most important thing in a language is to learn as many of these as you can. In my revision timetables, you may have noticed that I didn't give any time specifically for languages. That's because it's inefficient to try and spend an entire day trying to learn a language. Instead, you should do 30 minutes a day every day until the GCSEs. If you do 30 minutes a day for 4 months, you'll have spent 60 hours in total revising it, which is enough to have learnt essentially every word on the specification. You need to remember that in all your exams, 99% of the words they use are in that specification. In my GCSE, only one mark was for a word outside the specification (it was in the listening exam) but there's no point learning extra Spanish outside of the specification just for one or two more marks.

The second most important thing in a language is conjugations. You cannot get a grade 8/9 unless you can confidently conjugate verbs into a minimum of three tenses – at least one past, one future and the present. It's important to be able to do this on the spot, especially for the speaking exam.

I did AQA GCSE Spanish so my advice here will be centred on this exam board, but will probably be very similar to other exam boards.

Your GCSE will be composed of four components – listening, speaking, reading and writing. Each exam is worth 25% and you won't sit all the papers at the same time – you'll sit the speaking exam a few weeks before the rest of your GCSEs.

Listening

Before they start playing the recordings, you get a few minutes to read through the paper. First, quickly skim through the paper and translate any Spanish questions which you don't immediately understand. Then look at the multiple choice questions and translate the different options into English so you can answer them more easily in the exam.

You'll hear each question twice, with a 10 second pause in between for you to write it down – try to use this time to write rather than writing while they're talking. Also, keep listening right to the end of each track, as they often contradict themselves at the end or change their mind.

If you hear a track twice and you're still not sure about the answer, just write something down sensible because there's a chance it could be right and there's no negative marking.

Speaking

There are three parts of the speaking exam – role play, photo card and conversation. While your conversation has to be done completely on the spot, they'll give you 10 minutes of preparation time for the role play and photo card. Spend 2–3 minutes on your role play and the other 7–8 minutes on your photo card. Use a range of tenses and give opinions and reasons in this. It's ok to slip-up a bit or to go "umm" a few times but try to sound as confident as you can. Also, try and use the accent of the language you're doing, because examiners don't like it much if you use a British accent while speaking their language.

Reading

The most important thing to remember in the reading is that you will not understand everything, but that doesn't mean you can't get almost every question correct. You have to use the context of the text to help you understand what it's saying. You need to be able to spot different types of words, like nouns and adjectives, and it's extremely important to know as many verbs as you can from the specification so you have a basic idea of what's happening. Also, try to look for cognates as much as you can. These are words that look the same as the English, for example in Spanish, problema is problem.

Also, make sure you leave enough time for the translation section at the end which is worth more marks than any other question in the paper. In this, you have to translate a small passage from your foreign language to English. Make sure you translate it, a sentence at a time rather than word by word, as other languages often have a different word order to English. Look out for different tenses; they'll almost certainly use at least three types of tenses. At the end reread the entire translation to ensure that it makes perfect sense when read in English. If it doesn't, make little changes that don't affect the meaning but help it to sound more natural.

Writing

The most important thing in the first two sections of the writing paper is to cover every single bullet point, as you lose at least 4 marks for every bullet point you miss. If you don't understand what one of the bullet points want, don't worry as you always get a choice between 2 essays, so you can just choose the other one. To maximise your marks, use varied vocab and at least 4 different tenses. After you're done, check through your essay, looking out for: verb conjugations, adjective agreements and spellings/accents. These are minor problems but are easy to fix so you can stop yourself from losing silly marks.

Again, make sure you leave enough time for the translation, this time from English to your foreign language. The same ideas apply as in the reading. Translate it a sentence at a time, not word for word. Think about what the sentence means and then write that in your language, thinking about the word order. For example in English, the adjective comes before the noun, but in Spanish the adjectives come after the noun.

BUSINESS STUDIES

How well you do in business studies has far less to do with how much you remember going into the exam, but on how well you can make points for and against a business decision on the spot for a business you've never seen before with limited context.

My business studies exam was with the exam board CIE, and in my spec there was a clear way to gain almost all the marks. Paper 1 would have 8 marks for definitions, 8 marks for naming advantages/disadvantages of a certain thing, and would have a 4 mark question and two 6 mark questions. To get all 4 marks, you have to make 2 relevant points and give 2 pieces of "application", which is basically quoting a relevant piece of information from the context given. To get all the 6 marks, you had to make points, give application, analyse your points and make a conclusion.

However, most of you will probably be doing AQA Business, which covers basically the same content but has a different exam layout. The essentials remain the same though, a large mark question will say "Recommend whether ___ should _____?" and you need to be able to make an argument for why they should do that, then an argument for why they maybe shouldn't do that, and finally a conclusion saying what you think and why.

If you do AQA, you also have an advantage in that your papers are split by topic. Paper 1 is more business operation and human resources while paper 2 is more marketing and finance. CIE is different as you could get any topic in either paper, the difference is that Paper 1 is full of questions between 2 and 6 marks long, while all Paper 2 questions are either 8 mark or 12 mark essay questions.

In business studies, whichever exam board you do, it's important to do multiple past papers so you get a feel of what the exam paper will be like and you know how to answer questions. Also, because of the new specification there aren't many past papers so if you do AQA or Edexcel, you should buy the Business workbooks from CGP. However, I wouldn't recommend the revision guides as you need broad knowledge of the subject to be able to make an argument for and against anything the exam could throw at you.

COMPUTER SCIENCE

Computer science is very similar to a science in that it's basically just learning facts from the textbook. If you do OCR or AQA, I would definitely recommend buying the CGP GCSE computer science workbooks for practice, especially as there aren't enough past papers due to the new specification.

If you do CIE like I did, the specification has barely changed in the new GCSE so just do past papers from the old specification and mark them more harshly.

For computer science, make sure that you learn how things (like a printer or a sensor and microprocessor) work in perfect order, as in exams they'll often ask you to recite it for large mark questions.

The good thing about computer science is that it's similar to normal sciences. As long as you've thoroughly revised the textbook so you know all the information, and you've done a couple of past papers so you understand the formatting, you will easily be able to get over 80%.

Computer Science in my year was still graded A* to G. I got A and missed the A* by just 2 marks. This was highly disappointing as I was aiming for a clear A* in it. In retrospect I would urge you to use the main, detailed textbook rather than the revision guide.

GEOGRAPHY

Geography is a very hard GCSE. The theory content itself is as much as any other GCSE, but on top of that are several case studies which you have to learn. This massively increases the content you have to learn. I had worked hard in Geography but this is one subject I was not expecting a Grade 9. So I was thrilled when I did achieve that. The advantage to this is that the grade boundaries are quite low. In my GCSE (2018), a 9 was 73%, a 7 was 57% and a 4 was only 35%.

For geography, all questions which are 6 marks or above should reference a case study for maximum marks. This means that for geography, your theory needs to be very good and you need to try to remember as many facts from your case studies as you can. In the exam, whenever you see a 6, 9 or 12 mark question, first write down any relevant information you remember to answer the question. And then, if the question is about a city in an LIC, for example, name the one that you studied in class and give a relevant statistic.

Additionally, in geography, they'll often show a picture and ask you to answer a question based on it. Make sure to use the source. It may sound silly but many people know a lot of information about the topic so they quickly write down a perfect answer, before realising that they didn't even use the source. If you don't use it, you'll be severely marked down.

Paper 3 geography is a little more complicated. There's a pre-release booklet and a fieldwork section. Do past papers and specimen papers for this so you know the sort of questions they could ask about your fieldwork. Don't try to memorise the pre-release booklet because that'll be given to you in the exam. Instead, just analyse it and make some guesses as to what the 12 mark question at the end could be. Then make some sample answers and ask your teacher to mark them. If one of your questions does come up, you'll be able to answer it easily and more quickly. But don't try to give a prepared answer if the question is looking for something different. To my surprise I scored the highest marks in Geography Paper 3 in my school year.

Finally, make sure you pay attention in geography. It's far more important than in subjects such as maths or science because in geography if the teacher is going through a case study and you don't have all the notes, you won't have all the necessary material to do the exam, whereas in science everything you need is in the textbook.

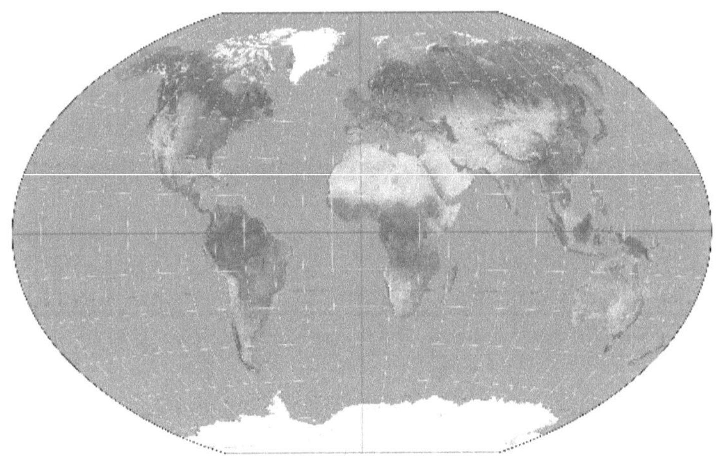

Exam Technique

In the end, revising and learning don't matter if you don't know how to answer the exam questions. Especially with the new GCSEs, exam technique has become much more important.

The new GCSEs, especially sciences, place huge importance on application. In fact, around 40% of the marks in a GCSE science exam are from applying your knowledge to an unknown situation. There's also "Working Scientifically" questions which are often very difficult because they require you to think about a practical, focusing on a certain aspect of it, such as the danger to yourself from doing it. These are also new with the GCSE change. All this means that it's no longer good enough to just memorise the textbook without understanding what it's saying, like it used to be.

APPLICATION QUESTIONS

These questions are based on the knowledge you have acquired, but are disguised so that it's not immediately obvious what it wants you to say.

This is where mind mapping comes in handy. This gives you an organised thought process so you can pick out the correct pieces of information from your memory. Some people create mental mind-maps naturally while revising, however some students, like me, don't.

Here's an easy way to tell: if a good mind mapper comes across a tricky question, they'll think about which topic the question would be under. Then which sub-topic from that topic it would come under, then they can answer the question because they've narrowed what they need to write down to 1 chapter. Someone who doesn't naturally mind map would look at the question and then just spend a few minutes racking their brain to try and think of an answer to write down. What's worse is that you could write something correct down, but it doesn't answer the question because it's from the wrong topic.

So, what can you do if you don't naturally mind map? At the end of each study session, before you get up from your chair, just remind yourself of the subject, topic and sub-topics that you covered so that your mind groups the information you just learnt under that topic. Try learning the names of all the chapters – it doesn't have to be the exact name – as long as you have a general idea of what information is in what chapter.

SILLY MISTAKES

The most common reason for a silly mistake is not reading the question properly. This could either be because of misreading a word in the question, or more commonly, being in such a rush to write the answer that you skim read the question and miss a bit out. If you've made many mistakes in the past due to misreading questions, consider reading every question twice. I would always read it once carefully, then write my answer, then read it again just to be sure before moving on to the next one.

Alternatively, you could try underlining key words in the question in order to force yourself to read the question more closely. This is faster than double reading it and also prevents you from skim reading the question.

Make sure to read the entire question, from the first word to the last. Never assume you know what it's going to say because you've seen a similar question multiple times before.

Another common silly mistake is simply not answering the exact question they're asking. This could either happen because you misinterpret the question, or because you started off answering it, but went off track at a tangent to the original question. This is most common in English exams where you have to write a long essay. In order to prevent yourself from doing this, refer back to the question every paragraph in an English essay. This also shows the examiner that you're definitely answering the question, making it easier for him to give you marks. When you do this, use the exact wording of the question to make it blatantly obvious to the examiner that you're sticking to the question asked.

PRESSURE

Many exam mistakes are made because of all the pressure on you to do well in it, along with the time constraints making you more scared. Firstly, remember that exam pressure is natural, you should feel nervous to an extent and a little adrenaline will help you write faster and will keep you motivated and concentrated. The problem occurs if you get too scared and start to panic. Then you stop being able to think, which makes you panic even more. This creates a vicious cycle which you need to end consciously.

Do all your exam preparation well in advance, allowing you to have some time to relax the night before and the day of the exam. Any revision you do the night before should just be simple reading rather than any intense revision. It's immeasurably more important to get a good night of sleep the night before than to fit in 1 more hour of revision, that is unless you've left all your revision to the very last minute.

When you get to school, everyone else will be talking about the exam, testing each other and cramming information but doing all this will only increase nerves. If you're going to do anything, just sit down and read from the textbook. A worst case scenario is if someone tests you and you momentarily forget the answer, it'll send you into a panic. Instead be confident. Talk to a friend about a non-exam related topic before you enter the exam hall, preferably something positive. The best thing you can do at this stage is just be happy because the more positive your outlook, the less likely you are to panic soon which is good for your exam.

Time pressure is a major problem in some subjects, especially essay based subjects like English. In these, always follow the allocated time for each subject as they're designed to give you an equal amount of time per mark. A general rule in GCSE is a mark a minute. If a science paper is 100 marks, you should be halfway within 45 minutes, leaving 5 minutes spare for checking. If 45 minutes have passed and you're not halfway yet, you need to pick up the pace. Ensure you bring a watch into the exam as invigilators aren't allowed to tell you when 45 minutes are up.

Also, never spend too much time on a single question. If you can't think of an answer to a question within 2 minutes, put a dot or star next to it and move on. Then at the end, go back to all the dotted/starred questions and see if you can remember.

You must properly check the paper again and again until the invigilator says "Pens down." Checking an exam paper is probably the most boring thing in the world, but it would be a shame for all your revision to be wasted because you couldn't be bothered to recheck your paper in the actual exam. When checking your paper, first read the question, then carefully read your answer and ask yourself if it properly answers the question.

After the Exams

After the GCSEs you get a very long, well deserved summer holiday. After all that hard work it's time to chill out. Books away. Time to do so many things which you wanted to but didn't have the time. Play on the Xbox for hours, hang out with friends all day. Sleep late and sleep till noon!

It is also the ideal time to get some work experience and build your CV. I did the Duke of Edinburgh Silver award expedition at this time. You may at this stage know or not know what you would like to do later in life. So, getting work experience in any field may be beneficial. Work experience can range from 3 to 5 days. Your school should help in arranging some but you can find one yourself. For example, you could spend some time at your parents work place. Or you could try a charity shop who are often looking for volunteers. Most businesses are happy to provide a few days of work experience to aspiring young people. You could try a care home or even a farm.

A LEVEL CHOICES

There have been recent changes in the A levels as well. Now the schools are often restricting students to 3 subjects at A levels rather than 4 to 5 which was common before. Additionally, other qualifications have gained importance like the EPQ – Extended project Qualification. The EPQ is also liked by many universities as it shows a different kind of learning style. It's your choice of topic, in which the research is done on your own and you come up with a finished presentation. There is a large element of self-learning which universities like.

Coming down from 10 or 11 subjects at GCSE to just 3 is very difficult. There are some subjects which you like and do not want to give up. If you have a career choice in mind then then there are certain subjects which are more useful than others.

If you put your subjects down in Year 11, you are more than likely to change them as the months go by and your interests change. The good thing is most schools are flexible and allow you to change. I was allowed to start my Y12 with 5 subjects and then drop some after the teaching began and I had a better idea of what I want. The choices I had put down in the summer time were Maths, Further Maths, Physics, Chemistry and Biology. Later I dropped Biology and Chemistry, and took Economics instead.

THE RESULTS DAY

The results come out in late August. A useful advice is not to go on holiday on that day and for a week after that. It's best to collect the results in person from school in case you want to send any papers for remarking as there is a short window to apply. On the day of the results you can meet your teachers and take advice about rechecking or subject choices etc. Also, the subject teachers have the detailed results i.e. exact marks break up for each paper. The students only get to know the grades. So, the teachers can check that and advice you accordingly. If your marks are just a few points below the grade boundary you have a chance of grade change in rechecking. If your marks are way off the grade boundary rechecking may not be beneficial, and even detrimental as you could fall down a grade.

In my case I got A in Computer Science which has 2 papers. I was only 2 marks below the grade boundary for A* so I sent both papers for rechecking. This does cost £38 per paper but the money is refunded if there is a grade change.

Finally...

GCSEs are the first external exams and doing well in them will give you a sense of achievement. More than that you are equipped with a learning style which will help you in all future exams.

I hope you have found this book useful in some ways and all the best for your exams.